MINERALS AND HEAVY METALS

Jill Sherman

Enslow Publishing
101 W. 23rd Street
Suite 240
New York, NY 10011
USA
enslow.com

Words to Know

circuit The path of an electric current.

disease Sickness.

mineral A natural substance that often comes from the ground.

natural resource Something from nature that people use.

preserve To keep safe for later use.

rust A reddish coating that forms on iron.

value The amount of money something is worth.

CONTENTS

Rock Resources

What good are rocks? You might think they have little use. But rocks contain minerals. Some even contain metals. These are great natural resources that we use all the time.

LETTERS

Building Blocks

Rocks are great for building. Red brick homes are sturdy. Stone walls stand strong. Builders mix minerals with rocks and water. They make concrete. It forms the base of many buildings.

Metal Hunt

Dig into rock. You may find metal. Metal is good for building. Look at some tools. See the nails and screws. Check out the pipes. They are all made of metal.

Kitchen Metals

Other tools are made from metal. Look in the kitchen. Forks, knives, and spoons are metal. So are the pots and pans. And so is the stove! Do you have canned soup or soda? Cans are metal too.

Fast Fact
Kitchen tools are made with stainless steel because it does not rust.

It's Electric

Unplug a lamp. What do you see? Metal! Electricity moves easily through metal. Wires and circuits have metal. They send messages. Our computers and devices would not work without metal.

FAST FACT
Copper is one of the most common metals used in wires.

Rock Riches

Gold and silver are rare metals. They are very valuable. Coins are made of different metals. All of our money has a gold value.

Mineral Gems

Stones have value too. Have you seen a diamond ring? A ruby necklace? Minerals may form colorful gems. They are used in jewelry.

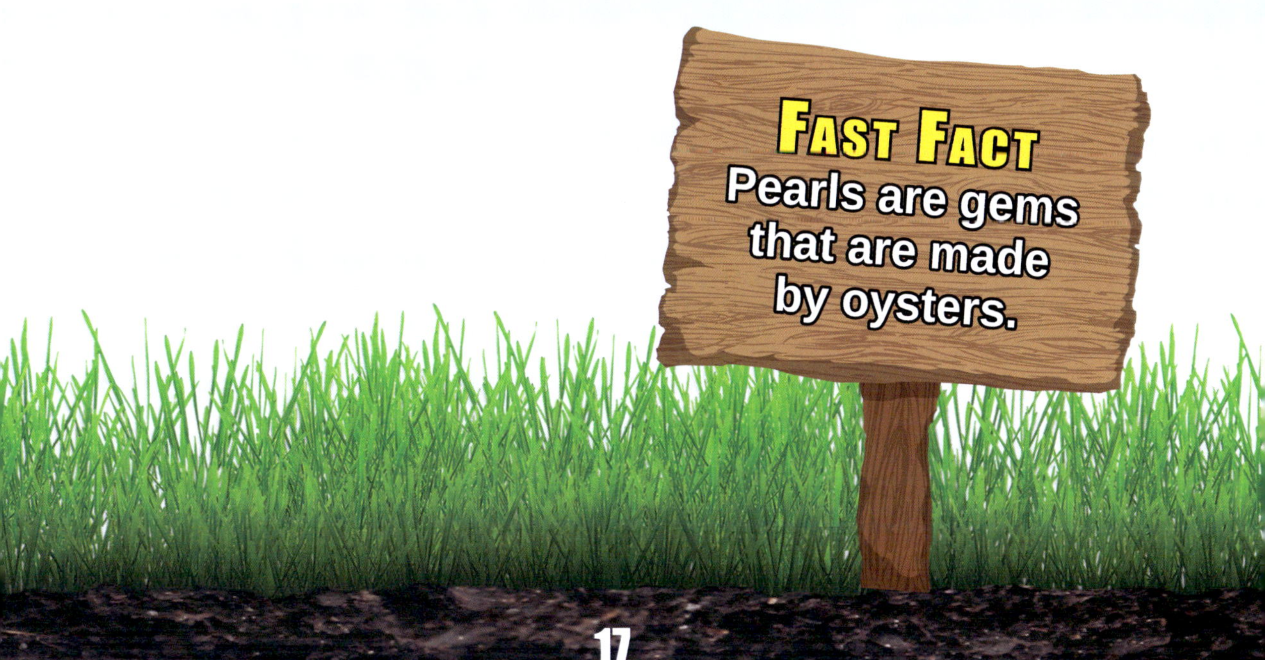

Body Minerals

Minerals keep us healthy. Salt is a mineral that you can eat. We use it to cook. It tastes good. It also preserves food to eat later.

Keeping Us Healthy

Our foods contain minerals. Calcium keeps bones strong. Iron carries oxygen to cells. Zinc helps fight disease. Minerals are a resource we could not live without.

Activity

Materials

cookie with visibly different ingredients, such as raisins, chocolate chips, or filling
paper plate
toothpicks

Rock Cookie

Procedure:

1. Rocks are like cookies. They are made of different ingredients, or minerals. Place a cookie on your paper plate.

2. Use your hands to crumble the cookie into many pieces.

3. With toothpicks, separate the cookie into all the different ingredients you can spot.

4. Sort the ingredients by size, shape, and color.

5. When a scientist looks at a rock, what kinds of things do you think he or she wants to know?

Learn More

Books

MacAulay, Kelley. *Why Do We Need Rocks and Minerals?* New York, NY: Crabtree Publishing. 2014.

Tomecek, Steve. *Dirtymeister's Nitty Gritty Planet Earth*. Washington, DC: National Geographic Kids. 2015.

Websites

Kids Health
kidshealth.org/en/kids/minerals.html
Understand the importance of minerals in the body.

Kids Love Rocks
kidsloverocks.com/index.html
An educational resource for young rock collectors.

Index

Published in 2018 by Enslow Publishing, LLC.
101 W. 23rd Street, Suite 240, New York, NY 10011

Library of Congress Cataloging-in-Publication Data

Names: Sherman, Jill., author.
Title: Minerals and heavy metals / Jill Sherman.
Description: New York : Enslow Publishing, 2018. | Series: Let's learn about natural resources | Includes bibliographical references and index.
Identifiers: LCCN 2017018168| ISBN 9780766091498 (library bound) | ISBN 9780766091474 (pbk.) | ISBN 9780766091481 (6 pack)
Subjects: LCSH: Mineralogy—Juvenile literature. | Minerals—Juvenile literature. | Metals—Juvenile literature.
Classification: LCC QE365.2 .S54 2018 | DDC 549—dc23

LC record available at https://lccn.loc.gov/2017018168

Printed in China

To Our Readers: We have done our best to make sure all website addresses in this book were active and appropriate when we went to press. However, the author and the publisher have no control over and assume no liability for the material available on those websites or on any websites they may link to. Any comments or suggestions can be sent by email to customerservice@enslow.com.

Photo Credits: Cover, p. 1 Cagla Acikgoz/Shutterstock.com; interior pages (soil, grass, sky) Andrey_Kuzmin/Shutterstock.com; interior pages (sign) johavel/Shutterstock.com; p. 4 Arsenie Krasnevsky/Shutterstock.com; p. 6 1000 Words/Shutterstock.com; p. 8 Joe Gough/Shutterstock.com; p. 10 TrotzOlga/Shutterstock.com; p. 12 sirtravelalot/Shutterstock.com; p. 14 Africa Studio/Shutterstock.com; p. 16 Hayati Kayhan/Shutterstock.com; p. 18 279photo Studio/Shutterstock.com; p. 20 Monkey Business Images/Shutterstock.com.